ITALY

UNPACKED

Clive Gifford

First published in 2013 by Wayland
Copyright © Wayland 2013

Wayland
338 Euston Road
London NW1 3BH

Wayland Australia
Level 17/207 Kent Street
Sydney, NSW 2000

Editors: Annabel Stones and Elizabeth Brent
Designer: Peter Clayman
Cover design by Matthew Kelly

Dewey number: 945'.09312–dc23

ISBN 978 0 7502 7727 3

Printed in China

10 9 8 7 6 5 4 3 2 1

Picture acknowledgements: All images, including cover images and graphic
elements, courtesy of Shutterstock except: p5 © Luca Zennaro/epa/Corbis
(br); p7 © 1001nights/iStock (b); p10 © carterdayne/iStock (tl); p11 © Sjo/
iStock (tr), © Bloomberg via Getty images (r); p12 © SerafinoMozzo (br); p13
© igorDutina (tl); p14 © Bloomberg via Getty images (l); p19 © Peter Barritt/
SuperStock/Corbis (tr); p21 © Daniel Dal Zennaro/epa/Corbis (l); p24 ©
Angelafoto/iStock (r), © Angelafoto (l); p25 © Massimo Merlini/iStock (t); p28
© Lifesizeimages/iStock (tl), © Francis G. Mayer/Corbis (tm)

The website addresses (URLs) included in this book were valid at the time of
going to press. However, it is possible that contents or addresses may
change following the publication of this book. No responsibility for any such
changes can be accepted by either the author or the Publisher.

Wayland is a division of Hachette Children's Books, an Hachette UK company.
www.hachette.co.uk

Contents

Italy: Unpacked

Welcome to Italy, a boot-shaped country full of phenomenal history and culture sticking out into the Mediterranean Sea. Once the centre of the Roman Empire, it was the biggest and most powerful ancient civilization the world had ever seen. Italy today is packed full of astonishing art, amazing architecture and spectacular scenery. So, if you want to learn about leaning towers, spy the world's sleekest sports cars and check out some of Europe's most amazing foods and inventions, you've come to the right place!

Fact file

Flag:

Area: 301,340km²
Population: 61.5 million
Capital city: Rome
Land Borders: 1,899.2km with six countries
Currency: The Euro

Useful Phrases

Ciao - Hello (informal)
Grazie tante - Thanks very much
Parlo poco Italiano - I speak a little Italian
Buona giornata - Have a nice day
Scusi, dov'è il bagno? - Excuse me, where's the toilet?
Quale è il suo nome? - What is your name?
Prego - You're welcome.
Non capisco - I don't understand.

A famous Italian tongue twister is:

"Trentatré trentini entrarono a
Trento tutti e trentatré trotterellando"

Thirty three people from Trento entered
the city, all thirty three waddling!

CITY PASS
CITY PASS 2
CITY PASS 3

There is a ban on building sandcastles
on the beaches of Eraclea, near Venice.
You can be fined 250 euros if you get
out your bucket and spade.

In 2008, Vittorio Innocente set a new world record
for cycling underwater, pedalling his bike 66.5m
in the Ligunan Sea close to the city of Genoa.

The Romans

In the 3rd century BCE, the small state of Rome captured its first foreign territory, Sicily, the largest island in the Mediterranean. The next 350 years saw the Romans expand their territory greatly. With a powerful and disciplined army conquering all before them, the Romans built an enormous empire that stretched throughout much of Europe and North Africa. At its largest, it covered an area of 6.5 million km^2.

The Pont du Gard aqueduct is 275m long and almost 50m high.

Roman Engineering

The Romans were masterful engineers who made great use of the arch and strong concrete. They built a range of structures, from bridges and aqueducts to carry fresh water, to famous buildings like the Pantheon in Rome, that exists to this day. Towns and cities were linked by networks of well-built, straight roads. At the empire's peak, some 400,000km of roads existed, including the Appian Way linking Rome to Brindisi in southeastern Italy. It also encouraged farmers to combine their land, creating larger farms.

Trajan's Forum in Rome was bigger than two soccer pitches.

Roman feasts featured some outrageous dishes including flamingo tongues, cow udders stuffed with sea urchins and stuffed dormice rolled in honey. Many dishes were covered in garum, a pungent sauce made from rotting fish intestines.

Roman Settlements

Roman cities featured advanced sewage systems, public baths and meeting places and markets. Trajan's Forum in Rome, for example, held spaces for more than 150 shops, and was one of the world's first shopping malls. Many poorer Romans lived in *insulae* apartment buildings whilst wealthier subjects lived in larger *domus* or in countryside villas. Some wealthy homes had mosaic-tiled floors and central heating systems called hypocausts which channelled hot air from a furnace under floors and up walls.

Roman soldiers marched rapidly, up to 35km a day.

Life and Death

The Romans made many medical advances, including performing caesarean section operations to remove a baby safely if there were complications during childbirth. Some of their cures, though, were less successful such as using earwax to soothe bites and mouse brains as toothpaste. The Romans also delighted in bloodthirsty gladiatorial games held in large stadia called amphitheatres and featuring men battling with wild animals or each other, often to the death.

Rome: The Eternal City

Exciting, chaotic and historic, Italy's capital city is a vibrant tangle of busy streets where modern buildings rub shoulders with ancient art and architecture. As the centre of the mighty Roman Empire, Rome was the most powerful city in the world for 700 years. Today, it remains a major world city attracting more than 7 million visitors a year.

Seven Hills

Rome started out as a crossing over the River Tiber but developed into a large settlement built over seven low-lying hills. By 50BCE, its population had passed one million. No city would match it in size for over 1,800 years. The Romans left behind awesome structures such as the Colosseum where gladiatorial games were held in front of enormous crowds.

Many of Rome's bridges crossing the Tiber are hundreds of years old.

At night, the Trevi Fountain lights up.

Swiss Guards have been guarding Vatican City since 1506.

Vatican City

Rome contains a separate nation, Vatican City. This is the world's smallest country and home to the Pope, the leader of the Roman Catholic Church. The Vatican also hosts the world's only ATM cash machine with instructions in Latin, as well as thousands of art treasures housed in its lavish museums. These are all guarded by the world's smallest army – the 110-strong Swiss Guard.

Fountains of Knowledge

Rome has 280 fountains including the spectacular Trevi Fountain (completed in 1762). The fountain is trawled every fortnight for the coins thrown in for good luck by tourists – as much as £740,000 is recovered and donated to charity each year. Rome is also home to many important libraries, research centres and universities. Its first university, La Sapienza, opened in 1303 and is now one of the largest in the world, with over 140,000 students.

NO WAY!

Rome is home to around 300,000 stray cats. Anyone caught killing a stray is fined 10,000 euros.

Way to Go

I taly has a fast, efficient train service running on 20,255km of track, 130 airports and almost half a million kilometres of roads. It won't take you long to spot some seriously sporty vehicles racing along - Italians love their fast cars. Some police forces are even equipped with top-of-the-range Lamborghini sports cars, so it's handy that certain *autostrade*, or motorways, have a top speed limit of 150km/h (93mph). Vrooom!

NO WAY!

In 2012, a 1962 vintage Ferrari 250 GTO was sold for a cool US$35 million. Only 39 of these classic cars were built.

Gondoliers

The only motor vehicles in Venice are motorboats and *vaporetto* water taxis. The entire city is built on a network of 100 islands, and more than 150 watery canals form its streets. Gondoliers work these routes, propelling their 11m-long, flat-bottomed boats using a single oar. Becoming one of the 425 licenced gondoliers in Venice is no easy task. There are over 400 hours of lessons and a tough exam to pass.

A gondolier moves forward and steers with his oar, called a *rèmo*.

Two Wheelers

Head into an Italian town or city and you'll see plenty of motor scooters zipping around. These are small, light motorbikes with a flat floor to place your feet on. There are more than five million scooters in Italy. Most are seen in rush hour in the cities, as they are the commuter vehicle of choice. Lambretta and Vespa (meaning wasp in Italian) are the most popular brands, both producing their first scooters in the late 1940s.

A classic Ferrari Dino supercar. Top speed: 235km/h.

Classic Cars

Italy's massive motor vehicle industry produces over 790,000 cars a year and is dominated by Fiat, a company whose factory in Turin boasts a complete car test track on its roof. However, Italian hearts beat faster when an Alfa Romeo, a Lamborghini, a Maserati or a Ferrari roars past. These sports car makes are world-renowned, especially Ferraris with their *rosso corsa* (racing red) paint job and distinctive bonnet badge featuring a prancing horse.

A scooter rally travels through the town of Verucchio, near Rimini.

Fiat 500L cars are built on a giant production line.

Food Glorious Food

If you think Italians are a nation of pasta and pizza lovers... you'd be right! No one eats more pasta than the people of Italy - over 25kg of pasta per person per year, enough for more than 120 meals. There are more than 350 different varieties of pasta, from thin *linguine* to tennis-racquet-shaped *racchette*, as well as plenty of different sauces to serve them with. Not all pasta is yellow. Some is coloured with spinach or, in the case of *pasta nera*, the ink from squid or cuttlefish that turns it black!

Pizza The Action

Breads with toppings on have existed since the time of the Etruscans, who lived in Italy before the Romans. However, the modern pizza is thought to have originated in Naples in the 19th century. The Margherita pizza, made with mozzarella cheese, tomato sauce and basil, was named after Italy's Queen Margherita and its colours represent the nation's flag. The world's biggest pizza was made by Italian chefs in 2012 and measured a staggering 40m in diameter.

Traditional pizzas are baked in a stone oven heated by a wood fire.

A mouthwatering selection of antipasto starters to a meal.

Dinner Time

The Italians eat a wide range of foods, not just pasta and pizza. Beef and pork dishes are common, as is fish and seafood caught off Italy's 7,600km of coastline. Lunch is often the heaviest meal of the day and consists of a number of courses, starting with small dishes of olives, fish, cheese and meats known as *antipasto*. A common tradition before dinner is to take a leisurely stroll, known as *La Passeggiata*, where you may see neighbours and other people you know also out and about.

Tasty tubs of gelato. Italy even has a Gelato University near Bologna to teach ice-cream making skills.

Just Desserts

Italians love their desserts, known as *dolce*. These can be as simple as fresh fruit or crispy *biscotti* (biscuits) or complex layered puddings like *tiramisu* or *Zuppa Inglese*. Italian *gelato* (ice cream) comes in hundreds of flavours.

La Bella Figura

The Italians believe in a concept called *La Bella Figura* (the beautiful figure). This is not just about how you dress but also about your posture, confidence and politeness in other people's company. Italians don't do saggy trackies, shell suits or onesies. They are amongst the best-dressed people in Europe and the Italian fashion industry is large and influential.

NO WAY!

Famous Italian fashion designer, Giorgio Armani designed the uniforms for the Italian Air Force!

Luxury cashmere clothing is made at the Brunello Cucinelli factory near Perugia.

Major Industry

Fashion, clothing and footwear are major industries in Italy. They directly employ around half a million people all over the country, producing and selling clothes to keep Italians and visitors well-dressed. In 2013, Italy sold approximately 44 billion euros worth of fashion abroad, making it one of the country's biggest exports.

Marvellous Milan

This large, bustling city has a long history of silk and clothing production stretching back to the Middle Ages. Today, it is thought of as the centre of the Italian fashion industry. Many of Italy's largest fashion houses, including Armani, Missoni and Prada, have their headquarters in Milan. Twice a year, in spring and autumn, the city also hosts some of the world's biggest fashion shows. More than 120 different collections of clothing are unveiled during Milan Fashion Week.

Family Fashion

In 1965, Luciano Benetton sold a bicycle to buy a secondhand knitting machine. His small collection of brightly coloured jumpers was so popular that his two brothers, Gilberto and Carlo, and his sister, Giuliana, joined him to form the Benetton Group. They opened their first shop in Belluno the following year.

A model wows with her Frankie Morello of Milan dress featuring the Leaning Tower of Pisa.

Benetton now has more than 6,000 stores in Italy and abroad.

Mountains and Volcanoes

When it comes to physical geography, Italy is a country of contrasts. Grassy plains, such as those in the Po Valley, and warm coastal beaches are found in some places, whilst around a third of the country is mountainous. One mountain range, the Apennines, runs a distance of 1,200km down the centre of the country. Its lower slopes are covered in trees, grasses and bushes, and 13 peaks reach over 2,000m in height.

The only way out of Italy by land is through the Alps.

The Alps

This giant mountain range runs through eight European countries including northern Italy. Monte Bianco (Mont Blanc) on Italy's border with France is the tallest mountain in the Alps with a height of 4,810.5m. Italy has hosted the Winter Olympics twice and used the Alps for skiing events, in 1956 at Cortina d'Ampezzo and in 2006 in Turin.

Buried Alive

Vesuvius is a volcano lying around 9km away from the city of Naples. Its most explosive eruption occurred in 79CE when it blew its top, sending out 75 million tonnes of ash and red-hot rock every minute for over six hours. The people of nearby towns Pompeii and Herculaneum were buried under 25m of ash, not to be discovered again for more than 1,700 years. Its eruption in 1906 damaged much of Naples whilst its last explosive activity, in 1944, destroyed four local villages.

Vesuvius looms in the distance over the ruins of Pompeii.

Red Hot

Mainland Europe's most active volcanoes are all found in Italy. Three – Etna, Vesuvius and Stromboli – have erupted in the past century. Etna is located on Sicily and has erupted many times in the past 50 years. In 2008, huge amounts of red-hot lava from the volcano travelled over 6.5km across the island. Stromboli forms a small island of the same name some 60km off the coast of the toe of Italy. It has been erupting almost constantly for about 2,000 years, throwing glowing lava fragments hundreds of metres into the air.

Mount Etna throws up red-hot lava during an eruption.

The Italian Arts

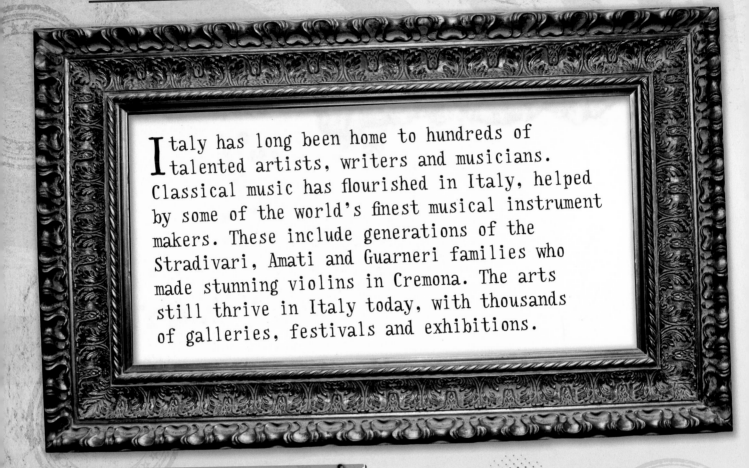

Italy has long been home to hundreds of talented artists, writers and musicians. Classical music has flourished in Italy, helped by some of the world's finest musical instrument makers. These include generations of the Stradivari, Amati and Guarneri families who made stunning violins in Cremona. The arts still thrive in Italy today, with thousands of galleries, festivals and exhibitions.

Mad Museums

Italy has over 3,300 museums. Whilst some, such as the Museum of Contemporary Art in Naples and the Uffizi in Florence, are world-famous, others are quirky and less well-known. There's an olive oil museum in Torgiano, for example, a museum devoted to water taps in San Maurizio d'Opaglio and an accordion museum in Castelfidardo. There's even a waxworks museum in Florence, called La Specola, which is devoted to victims of the Black Death – gruesome!

NO WAY!

In 1564, the Church decided to cover up some of the nude figures painted by Michelangelo! They asked artist Daniele da Volterra to paint underwear on the pictures.

The Sistine Chapel is now visited by 5 million tourists every year.

Opera

It's not all large men and ladies, singing their hearts out. Opera is theatrical drama, telling a story set to music, and Italy is its home. The first operas came out of Florence in around 1600. These were followed by famous operas written by Italian composers such as Verdi, Rossini and Puccini whose works included Madame Butterfly and La Bohème.

Michelangelo

One of Italy's most famous artists, Michelangelo worked in Florence, Bologna and Rome. He was a brilliant sculptor and painter and his masterpieces include the statue of David, and the astonishing ceiling of the Sistine Chapel in Vatican City. He was originally asked just to paint the 12 apostles of Jesus on the ceiling but ended up spending over four years (1508-1512) suspended on a scaffold to produce a series of scenes featuring 343 people.

Michelangelo's David is now in the Uffizi Gallery.

Today, there are still almost 50 opera houses like this one in Sicily to be found throughout Italy.

Calcio!

Football is Italy's national sport - most Italians are devoted followers of their national team's fortunes, and have a club they support as well. In 1999, one club, Fiorentina, even sold cans of air taken from their stadium to fans! The Italians call football *Calcio* from a 16th-century version of the sport played in Italy by 27-a-side teams.

NO WAY!

In a tense 1938 World Cup semi-final against Brazil, Italy's Giuseppe Meazza went to take a penalty kick and his shorts fell down! Cool as a cucumber, Meazza held them up with one hand and scored the penalty. Italy won the game!

The Azzuri

The Italian national team are nicknamed the *Azzuri* after the azure blue shirts they have worn since 1911. Italy have only once failed to qualify for the World Cup (in 1958) and have won the competition four times. Their last triumph, in 2006, saw the entire nation rejoice. Italian legends include Gianluigi Buffon – the world's most expensive goalkeeper – who cost £32.5 million in 2001, and Paolo Maldini, who played over 900 games for AC Milan.

'Gigi' Buffon has been voted Serie A's best keeper nine times.

Serie A

One of the greatest leagues in world football, Serie A has long been home to many of the world's best players and clubs. The 20 teams compete from September to May to win the *Scudetto* (shield). Top teams include Napoli, AC Milan, Internazionale (also known as Inter Milan) and Juventus, based in Turin, who have won the league more than any other side.

AC Milan's Stephan El Shaarawy playing against Inter Milan.

The mighty San Siro stadium, home to both Inter Milan and their fierce rivals, AC Milan.

Fans and Derbies

Derby matches between local rivals, such as the derby between Sampdoria and Genoa, especially excite fans. Some great rivals share a stadium, for example, Lazio and Roma both call the Olympic Stadium in Rome their home. Football fans attend games and follow their team's fortunes on the television and the radio. They often play casual games themselves, either full 11-a-side matches or an 8-a-side version of football called *calciotto*.

North and South

Italy is a mountainous and hilly country, but that hasn't stopped several million Italians from farming the land. There are over 1.6 million farms and smallholdings in Italy. More than 70% of these are devoted to growing crops. Italian industry is concentrated in the north of the country although oil refineries, chemicals and plastics companies can be found near ports in the south.

Bottles and Bouquets

Many Italian farmers grow wheat, maize or vegetables including tomatoes, soybeans and sugar beet. The warm climate in much of central and southern Italy has allowed it to become one of the world's leading producers of fruits, such as oranges, lemons, peaches and apricots. Many people also grow olives or flowers, and vineyards are found throughout the country.

Around one fifth of all the wine drunk in the world is produced in Italy — that's about 6.6 billion bottles a year!

NO WAY!

A massive food fight is staged every year in the Italian city of Ivrea. Over half a million oranges are imported from Sicily for the townspeople to throw at each other - juicy!

Industry

Italy imports most of the raw materials it needs for its industries, which range from high-tech electronics and computing companies to more traditional ceramics, leather goods and clothing manufacturers. Whilst car-makers and companies making white goods tend to be giants, most manufacturing companies are small businesses employing 50 people or less. Some industries have struggled in recent times and unemployment is high, especially amongst younger people.

80,000 barrels of oil a day are processed at Milazzo in Sicily.

Solar panels in Italy produce enough power to light 127 million 100w light bulbs.

Power

Italy closed all its nuclear power stations by 1990 following the 1987 Chernobyl disaster in the Ukraine. Partly as a result, Italians pay more for their electricity than most people in the EU. Italy is now the second biggest solar power producer in Europe behind Germany and the world's seventh largest wind power user. It also generates almost a fifth of its electricity using hydroelectricity.

Everyday Life

Italy's 60 million inhabitants include over 4.5 million people originally from other countries. More than a million Romanians, as well as large numbers of Moroccans and Albanians, call Italy home. Most people in the country speak Italian, but almost half the population also speak a local or regional dialect. Over a million people on Sardinia speak the Sardinian language. Almost nine out of ten Italians are members of the Roman Catholic Church.

Superstitions

Italians have a number of superstitions. Never wrap gifts in purple wrapping paper, for example, as it is thought to bring bad luck, and be careful when giving flowers as yellow blooms symbolise anger and jealousy. The number 17 has been considered unlucky in Italy since Roman times because the Roman numerals for 17 (XVII) are an anagram of VIXI, Latin for 'I have lived' or 'my life is over'. Many Italian theatres don't have a 17th row or seats numbered 17.

NO WAY!

Most bridegrooms carry a piece of iron with them on their wedding day as it's believed it will ward off Malocchio - the evil eye (a sort of curse).

Three generations of an Italian family. There are 7.8 million people under 14 years old in Italy.

Family Life

Italians tend to be quite touchy-feely, and often greet close friends and family with a hug and a kiss on both cheeks. A common tradition is to tug a child's ears on their birthday. Each tug represents a year of the child's life. Family life is extremely important to Italians who attend festivals and events together. Many adult Italian children live with their parents until they get married.

Italian Weddings

Weddings are a big deal in Italy with large numbers of guests and much ceremony. In fact, certain traditions found in other parts of the world, like the bridal veil, paper confetti and diamond engagement rings, were invented there. You can expect a feast of food at the reception after the marriage ceremony, where the bride may carry a small satin bag, called *la borsa*, for guests to donate gifts of money. At some weddings, the groom's tie is cut into little pieces which are auctioned off, again with the proceeds going to the newlyweds.

Super Cities

Italy has 150 towns or cities with a population of more than 50,000. These include the capital city, Rome, the major industrial cities of Turin and Milan in the north, and smaller cities such as Bari and Pescara in the south. The walled city of Lucca has almost 100 churches and you can walk or cycle along the tops of its medieval walls. Here are three of Italy's super cities.

Florence

Built on the banks of the River Arno, Florence was a major wool and cloth-making town in medieval times. It became a powerful centre of Renaissance Europe and home to artists including Michelangelo and Botticelli. Many of the city's greatest artworks are housed in the mighty Uffizi gallery. Amongst its other standout sights are the bridges across the Arno topped with houses and jewellers' workshops, and the *Duomo*, the city's cathedral. Inside, visitors face the challenge of climbing 463 steps to reach the top of the church's giant dome which gives great views of the red tiled roofs of Florence.

Great views from the top of Florence's cathedral.

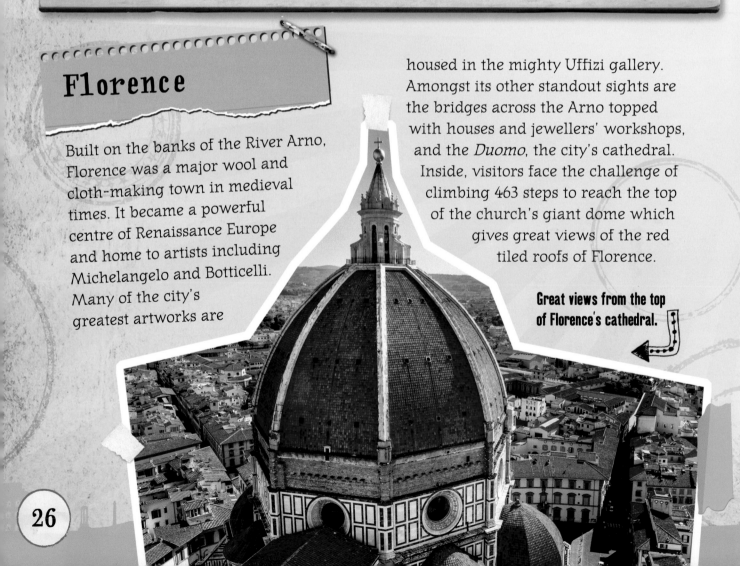

26

Palermo

The capital city of Sicily, Palermo was founded almost 2,800 years ago by Phoenician traders. The city has been ruled by many different empires including the Greeks, Normans, Arabs, the Swabians from Germany, the French and the Spanish. Menus in many Palermo restaurants are written out in five or more languages! Palermo is one of Italy's biggest ports, and handles 2 million passengers and around 5 million tonnes of cargo every year.

Naples

Naples is the industrial centre of southern Italy and the country's third largest city. It's perched on a broad bay 190km southeast of Rome, and is home to almost a million inhabitants. The first steam-powered ship in the Mediterranean Sea, the *Ferdinando I*, was launched from the city's dockyards in 1818, and Naples remains a busy port with around a million cruise liner passengers arriving each year. They flock to shop in its many markets and visit its famous old art galleries and theatres, including the Teatro di San Carlo, the oldest working opera house in the world.

NO WAY!

The Capuchin Catacombs in Palermo contain the preserved remains of about 8,000 mummified people, some in lifelike poses. Creepy!

Over 60,000 ships visit the port of Naples every year.

Italian Inventions

There have been plenty of ingenious Italians throughout the ages, but none more so than Leonardo da Vinci (1452–1519). He proved skilled at almost everything he attempted, from drawing, painting and sculpture to engineering and inventing. Da Vinci invented a lens grinding machine whilst also sketching out pioneering plans for ball bearings, armoured tanks, parachutes and a form of helicopter. Here are eight more devices for work and play that were originally developed or invented by Italians.

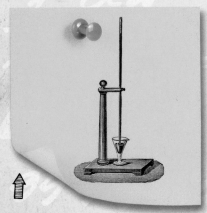

Barometer
Evangelista Torricelli (1643)

This device is used in weather forecasting to measure the pressure of the atmosphere.

Telephone
Antonio Meucci (1860)

The Florence-born Meucci demonstrated his *teletrofono* device in New York, USA, 16 years before Alexander Graham Bell famously made his first phone call.

Electroplating
Luigi Brugnatelli (1805)

The use of electricity to coat metals with a thin layer of gold, silver or another metal. It is used in making jewellery and cutlery.

Space hopper
Aquilino Cosani (1968)

This bouncy ball with handles has given millions of children fun in the garden.

Piano
Bartolomeo Cristofori (1700-1710)

Whilst working in Padua, Cristofori built the first pianos with hammers striking strings.

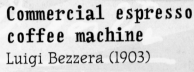

Commercial espresso coffee machine
Luigi Bezzera (1903)

Bezzera improved existing coffee machines to brew coffee quickly using hot water and steam under pressure.

Radio (practical radio transmissions)
Guglielmo Marconi (1896)

In 1901, Marconi became the first person to send a message via radio waves across the Atlantic Ocean.

NO WAY!

Thousands of pages of notes made by Leonardo da Vinci survive to this day. Most were made in backwards writing, decipherable by using a mirror.

A statue of Da Vinci looking thoughtful in Milan.

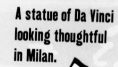

Crossword puzzle
Giuseppe Airoldi (1890)

The forerunner of today's crosswords was first published in an Italian magazine.

More information

Websites

http://www.italia.it/en/home.html
Italy's official tourism website is packed with information about the country.

http://www.italiansrus.com/
Read all about Italian customs and folk tales on this great site.

http://www.bbcgoodfood.com/content/recipes/cuisines/italian/
Dozens of mouthwatering recipes for Italian food can be found here.

http://www.delish.com/recipes/cooking-recipes/italian-recipes
And more here – from simple *crostini* (toasts with toppings) to delicious desserts.

http://www.google.com/culturalinstitute/collection/uffizi-gallery?projectid=art-project&hl=en-gb
Take a virtual tour of many Italian masterpieces housed at the Uffizi Gallery in Florence.

Apps

Fotopedia Italy A wide and varied selection of groovy photos and facts for your iPhone or iPad.

Italian Lessons and Flashcards Learn some key Italian words and phrases easily with this LangLearner Lessons app for all Android devices.

Mom's Italian Recipes Dozens of tasty recipes from Italy are available using this Android app.

3D Drag Race Start with a Fiat Punto and end up spending your race winnings on a Ferrari or Lamborghini in this simple drag racing game for Android devices.

Movies

Cinema Paradiso The story of a young boy from Sicily and his love of films and the cinema.

The Italian Job This classic British film, starring Michael Caine as a gangster trying to steal a haul of gold, is set largely in Turin.

Il Postino An exiled Chilean poet moves to a small Italian island and befriends the local postman.

Clips

http://www.youtube.com/watch?v=F_wY6cYGXp4
Watch the fast and furiously messy action at the Battle of the Oranges in Ivrea.

http://www.youtube.com/user/LoveSerieA
Catch all the latest Serie A action and highlights on this YouTube channel.

http://www.youtube.com/watch?v=Owp6eXHxo7Q
Let TV historian Adam Hart-Davis guide you through some of the stranger inventions and innovations the Romans brought to Britain.

http://www.youtube.com/watch?v=ATHL-7KfKLO
Watch an epic gondola race taking place in Venice in May 2012.

Books

Discover Countries: Italy by Kelly Davis (Wayland, 2012)

Food and Cooking in Ancient Rome by Clive Gifford (Wayland, 2010)

Leonardo and the Death Machine by Robert J. Harris (HarperCollins Children's, 2011)

The Real: Italy by Paolo Messi (Franklin Watts, 2013)

Rome: An Expanding 3D Guide by Kristyna Litten (Walker, 2012)

A World of Food: Italy by Jane Bingham (Franklin Watts, 2010)

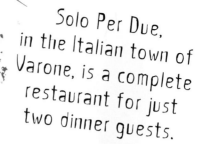

Solo Per Due, in the Italian town of Varone, is a complete restaurant for just two dinner guests.

Glossary

active volcano – A volcano which has erupted recently or is likely to erupt.

Black Death – A plague of disease which struck Europe in the 14th century and killed many millions of people.

commuters – People who travel from one place to another regularly, for example, from home to work and back each day.

decipherable – To be able to solve a code.

dialect – A version of a language spoken by a particular group of people.

exports – Goods or materials which are sent to another country for sale or for trade.

gladiatorial games – Entertainment held during the time of the Romans featuring wild animals and men fighting each other, sometimes to the death.

hydroelectricity – Using moving water to turn machines to generate electricity.

imported – To buy goods or materials in from other countries or regions.

inhabitants – People who live in a place.

manufacturing – Turning raw materials into a finished object or item.

Renaissance – A period of intense activity in the arts, learning and philosophy that began in Italy and spread through Europe in the 14th and 15th centuries.

smallholdings – A term used to describe a small farm, usually run by a single family.

unemployment – To be out of work and without a job.

Index

Unpacked

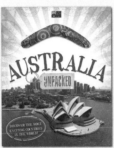

Australia
Australia: Unpacked
Exploration and Discovery
City Sights
Not All Desert
Aussie Animals
Long Distance Travellers
Go, Aussie, Go!
Mine Time
On the Coast
Native Australians
Aussie Tucker
Everyday Life
Coming to Australia

978 0 7502 7726 6

Brazil
Brazil: Unpacked
A World of Faces
Let's Go to Rio!
Viva Futebol!
Jungle Giant
Nature's Treasure Trove
Highways and Skyways
Bright Lights, Big Cities
Life, Brazilian Style
Looking Good
Arts for All
Adventurous Tastes
Prepare to Party!

978 0 7502 7997 0

France
France: Unpacked
The City of Light
Ruling France
Fruit of the Earth
Home and Away
Power and Progress
Grand Designs
Bon Appetit
The Arts
En Vacance
Made in France
Allez Sport
Life in France

978 0 7502 7728 0

India
India: Unpacked
From 0 to a Billion
Touring India
Everyone's Game
Wild Wonders
Rocks, Rivers, Rains
Life on the Land
High-tech, Low-tech!
Staggering Cities
Everyday India
Spice is Nice
Bollywood Beats
Bright Arts

978 0 7502 7725 9

Italy
Italy: Unpacked
The Romans
Rome: the Eternal City
Way to Go
Food Glorious Food
La Bella Figura
Mountains and Volcanoes
The Italian Arts
Calcio!
North and South
Everyday Life
Super Cities
Italian Inventions

978 0 7502 7727 3

Portugal
Portugal: Unpacked
Small Country, Big Story
Let's Play!
Holiday Hotspot
Sun, Sand and Serras
Island Magic
Charismatic Cities
Made in Portugal!
Country Corkers
Wild Times
Make Yourself at Home
Surf 'n Turf
Creative Culture

978 0 7502 7886 7

South Africa
South Africa: Unpacked
Three Capitals
The Land
Becoming South Africa
SA Sport
Farming
Rainbow Nation
Fabulous Food
Rich and Poor
Wild Life
Mineral Wealth
On the Coast
Holidays and Festivals

978 0 7502 7729 7

Spain
Spain: Unpacked
A World of Their Own
Fiesta Forever
On the Ball
Highlands and Islands
Sleepless Cities
Escape to the Country
Wild Spain
Spanish Life
All You Can Eat
Hola World!
Olé, Olé!
Eye-Popping Arts

978 0 7502 7730 3

WAYLAND
www.waylandbooks.co.uk